OWN YOUR DAY
OWN YOUR ROAR

7 Golden Keys Designed to Unlock Your Identity & Destiny

Inspired and written in partnership with my Best Friend, Constant Companion and Guide, Holy Spirit.

Copyright © 2023 by Korrie L Silver

Book publishing services by Opulent Books: www.OpulentBooks.net

ISBN: 978-1-916691-20-9

All rights reserved.

First edition 2023

No portion of this book may be reproduced in any form without written permission from the publisher or author, except as permitted by either Canadian or U.S. copyright law. This publication is designed to provide accurate and authoritative information regarding the subject matter covered. It is sold with the understanding that neither the author nor the publisher is engaged in rendering legal, investment, accounting, or other professional services. While the publisher and author have used their best efforts in preparing this book, they make no representations or warranties with respect to the accuracy or completeness of the contents of this book and specifically disclaim any implied warranties of merchantability or fitness for a particular purpose. No warranty may be created or extended by sales representatives or written sales materials. The advice and strategies contained herein may not be suitable for your situation. You should consult with a professional when appropriate. Neither the publisher nor the author shall be liable for any loss of profit or any other commercial damages, including but not limited to special, incidental, consequential, personal, or other damages.

Scriptures marked MSG are taken from THE MESSAGE, copyright © 1993, 2002, 2018 by Eugene H. Peterson. Used by permission of NavPress. All rights reserved. Represented by Tyndale House Publishers, Inc.

Scriptures marked AMP are taken from the AMPLIFIED BIBLE (AMP): Scripture taken from the AMPLIFIED® BIBLE, Copyright © 1954, 1958, 1962, 1964, 1965, 1987 by the Lockman Foundation Used by Permission. Lockman.org

Scriptures marked NKJV are taken from the NEW KING JAMES VERSION (NKJV): Scripture taken from the NEW KING JAMES VERSION®. Copyright© 1982 by Thomas Nelson, Inc. Used by permission. All rights reserved.

Scriptures marked ESV are taken from THE HOLY BIBLE, ENGLISH STANDARD VERSION (ESV): Scriptures taken from THE HOLY BIBLE, ENGLISH STANDARD VERSION ® Copyright© 2001 by Crossway, a publishing ministry of Good News Publishers. Used by permission.

Scriptures marked NIV are taken from the NEW INTERNATIONAL VERSION (NIV): Scripture taken from THE HOLY BIBLE, NEW INTERNATIONAL VERSION ®. Copyright© 1973, 1978, 1984, 2011 by Biblica, Inc.TM. Used by permission of Zondervan.

Scriptures marked TPT are from The Passion Translation®. Copyright © 2017, 2018, 2020 by Passion & Fire Ministries, Inc. Used by permission.
All rights reserved. ThePassionTranslation.com.

Scriptures marked NLT are taken from the HOLY BIBLE, NEW LIVING TRANSLATION (NLT): Scriptures taken from the HOLY BIBLE, NEW LIVING TRANSLATION, Copyright© 1996, 2004, 2007 by Tyndale House Foundation. Used by permission of Tyndale House Publishers, Inc., Carol Stream, Illinois 60188. All rights reserved. Used by permission.

Presented to: ....

From: ....

Date: ....

VIDEO SUMMARY

Want a video summary of this book that will help you make quick progress on your journey?
Go to:

www.ownyourdayownyourroar.com/7keys

DEDICATION

I dedicate this book to every fierce, faith-filled Lioness whose R.O.A.R. the world is eagerly waiting to hear.

My fellow Lionesses, our time is now!

Korrie L Silver

ACKNOWLEDGEMENTS

A special thank you to my dear sisters in Christ, Nicole Jansen-Lofton and Cassandra Lattin. They encouraged me in 2021 to contribute to the "Dare to be Different" Women's Devotional App. This endeavor became an early version of what is now **"Own Your Day, Own Your Roar: 7 Golden Keys Designed to Unlock Your Identity and Destiny."**

I also want to thank my dear sister and fellow author, Lindy Lewis, you are a constant source of creative inspiration. I am deeply honored by our journey together and your willingness to pray, share, challenge, sharpen and encourage me to become the most authentic version of myself!

CONTENTS

Golden Key One
We are Crafted in the Image of our Creator — 1

Golden Key Two
We are Called to Co-Create with our Creator — 21

Golden Key Three
We are Created to R.O.A.R. — 41

Golden Key Four
We are Commissioned to Fulfill a Unique Destiny — 69

Golden Key Five
We are Conceived to Co-create, Co-labor and Co-birth — 87

Golden Key Six
We are Charged to Humble Ourselves & to Surrender — 107

Golden Key Seven
We are Convoked to Release a Multi-Generational R.O.A.R. — 125

Hello & Welcome!

Own Your Day, Own Your Roar is a mission-based movement designed to inspire and challenge women to **Recognize, Own, Activate,** and **Release** their own unique sound. Walking out their God-given identity and destiny with integrity and confidence. Knowing that it is the Creator who is roaring through His Creation, co-creating with intent and excellence.

The 7 Golden Keys outlined in **Own Your Day, Own Your Roar** are designed to equip and empower entrepreneurially minded women who are both fierce and faith-filled, to unlock a multi-generational Remnant-R.O.A.R. and become the marketplace Lionesses they were created to be.

Throughout the Bible we see the significance and symbolism of gold used to unlock the depths of divine wisdom, worth, purity, wealth, power, and the Glory of God Himself! We often associate gold with its refining process where it is formed and purified in fire – just as we ourselves are purified by our Refiner's Fire.

The 7 Golden Keys shared in this book are to be used to refine and purify our lives so that the Golden Oil of Heaven can be seen in and through our lives, our identities and of course, our destinies.

Keys, allow us to unlock new doors, new dimensions, and step into new beginnings. Keys hold power.

In Isaiah 22:22 (NLT), it is written *"I will give him the key to the house of David - the highest position in the royal court. When he opens doors, no one will be able to close them; when he closes doors, no one will be able to open them."*

Keys have authority. As we learn to utilize these 7 Golden Keys, my prayer is that we will learn to unlock our own power and authority in Christ Jesus our Lord.

Consider utilizing this resource within your own community of sisters, as you learn to Own Your Roar together.

Korrie L Silver

Why Should I, Own My Day?

As we journey together through these 7 Golden Keys, I invite you to interact with each Key: to reflect, to seek deeper revelation, and, of course, to take responsibility for the release of your own creative R.O.A.R.—the sound that only you were designed to make.

Why Should I, Own My R.O.A.R.?

It is written in Psalms 139:16 (TPT) that *"You saw who you created me to be before I became me! Before I'd ever seen the light of day, the number of days you planned for me were already recorded in your book"*.

It is time for us to **Recognize, Own, Activate, and Release** who we were created to be!

Golden Key One

We Are Crafted in the Image of Our Creator

In Genesis 1:26-27 (ESV) it is written *"Then God said, "Let us make man in our image, after our likeness. And let them have dominion over the fish of the sea and over the birds of the heavens and over the livestock and over all the earth and over every creeping thing that creeps on the earth. So, God created man in his own image, in the image of God he created him; male and female he created them."*

Refining Your R.O.A.R.
- Reflection • Revelation • Responsibility

> **We are crafted — custom-made, authored, conceived — in the Image of our Creator.**

Creator God crafted us in His Own Image and Likeness with the direct mandate to steward and to create. As we come to know our Creator and accept Jesus Christ as our Lord and Savior, we begin to have this deep-seated hunger to understand the purpose for which we have been created.

In Colossians 3:10 (TPT), it is written *"For you have acquired new creation life which is continually being renewed into the likeness of the One who created you; giving you the full revelation of God."*

Our Creator crafted us in His Own Image and Likeness!

Some of you are called to birth Kingdom businesses, while others have inventions waiting to be brought to market. There are songs yet to be written, ministries to be launched, and prophetic words to be released. Your impact will reach communities, cities, and even nations. Throughout all these endeavors, you have the 'full revelation of God' as your mentor, coach, and guide.

Our destiny was determined 'ahead of time' and it is our birthright to be our Creator God's hands and feet here on earth. To bring Glory to His Name and establish His Kingdom on earth as it is in Heaven as it is written in Luke 11:2b *"Your kingdom come. Your will be done on earth as it is in heaven"* (NKJV).

It is vitally important now, more than ever before, that we **Recognize, Own, Activate** and **Release** our own unique identity and fulfill our God-given assignments and ultimately our God-given destinies. Each one of us was created on purpose, for a purpose.

The Time Is Now.

Can you perceive deep within your spirit the sense of urgency to discover and release your one-of-a-kind, custom-made sound? To breathe the air of purpose; to inhale identity and exhale destiny?

In Genesis 2:7 (NLT), it is written *"Then the Lord God formed the man from the dust of the ground. He breathed the breath of life into the man's nostrils, and the man become a living person".*

I invite you in this moment to pause, to inhale the reality of your identity; to exhale fear. To inhale the breath of life and exhale your pre-conceived notion of your destiny.

You were crafted on purpose, in the Image of the greatest Creator of all time!

It is time to know whose you are and seek His direction for your life.

In Romans 8:28-30 (TPT), it is written, "So we are convinced that every detail of our lives is continually woven together to fit into God's perfect plan of bringing good into our lives, for we are his lovers who have been called to fulfill his designed purpose. For he knew all about us before we were born, and he destined us from the beginning to share the likeness of his Son. This means the Son is the oldest among a vast family of brothers and sisters who will become just like him. Having determined our destiny ahead of time, he called us to Himself and transferred his perfect righteousness to everyone he called. And those who possess his perfect righteousness he co-glorified with his Son".

Key Takeaways

1. We are created on purpose, for a purpose.

2. We are crafted in His Image and Likeness to steward and to create.

3. Our identity and destiny matter. We must choose to do whatever it takes to discover our unique purpose and release our unique R.O.A.R.

In Deuteronomy 6:4-5 (NLT), we discover what is known as the Shema Prayer:

"Listen, O Israel! The Lord is our God, the Lord alone. And you must love the Lord your God with all your heart, all your soul, and all your strength".

The word 'listen' in Hebrew is the word 'Shema' which literally is translated to mean 'listen and obey'.

As an act of our genuine love for our Creator God, let us choose to listen and obey His Voice. He is revealing to us our unique identity and calling, so that we can fulfill His original intent and design for our individual lives. We are the carriers of His great love and Good News in the world today.

Creator God, the One whose Image we bear, we give you the highest Glory, Honor, and Praise! We are humbled to know that You, our Creator, long to co-create with us, Your Creation. We choose to 'listen and obey' Your great plan and purpose both individually and collectively; we commit to doing the work necessary to discover our R.O.A.R. and helping others to do the same.

In Jesus' Name, Amen.

The R.O.A.R. of Reflection, Revelation & Responsibility

How does the knowledge that you were made in the Image and Likeness of God realign how you see yourself?

Invite Holy Spirit to give you a fresh revelation of your personal identity in Christ. What is He saying to you?

How can you choose to partner with Holy Spirit to inhale your identity and exhale fear?

What is your unique, one-of-a-kind, custom-made sound? Define and describe it.

Use the space below to capture Creative AHA's.

Use the space below to capture Creative AHA's.

Golden Key Two

We Are Called to Co-Create With Our Creator

In Genesis 1:28 (NIV), it is written *"God blessed them and said to them, 'Be fruitful and increase in number; fill the earth and subdue it. Rule over the fish in the sea and the birds in the sky and over every living creature that moves on the ground.'"*

Refining Your R.O.A.R.
- Reflection • Revelation • Responsibility

> **We are called — imaged, designed, appointed — to co-create.**

The creative R.O.A.R. of the Lionesses at this time will dumbfound the enemy and bring tremendous Joy as well as Glory and Honor to the Roaring Lion of Judah!

One of the definitions for the word "roar", according to the Merriam-Webster online dictionary is to "laugh loudly".

I smile every time I think of this definition because prophetically, I believe that is exactly what we, the Daughters (Lionesses) of God are being called to do. I see us being called to the forefront of both business and ministry and being positioned to release a roar of laughter in the face of our common enemy.

In Genesis 3:15 (NLT), it is written
"And I will cause hostility between you and the woman, and between your offspring and her offspring..."

Co-creating, co-laboring,
co-birthing. This is our divine birthright, made in
His Image and Likeness to steward and
to create.

As we begin to discover and understand our
individual assignments and purpose, we will
begin to accept and own that our divine
birthright is to co-create, co-labor, and co-birth
with our beloved Creator.

What a privilege. What a responsibility.
What an honor!

Another definition of the word "roar" also
according to the Merriam-Webster online
dictionary is to "sing or shout with full force".
Did you hear that? To SING or SHOUT with
full force!

Not quietly. Not timidly. With FULL FORCE!
The enemy has been fighting to silence us for
too long.

I believe the Lion of Judah is roaring over each one of us right now, bringing freedom and victory to ourselves and our families. The sound of His Roar is establishing the work of our hands.

In Job 22:28 (NKJV), it is written, *"You will also declare a thing, and it will be established for you; so light will shine on your ways"*.

In Proverbs 24:3 (TPT) it is written, *"Wise people are builders – they build families, businesses, communities. And through intelligence and insight, their enterprises are established, and endure"*.

My challenge for you, is to understand exactly what is being *"established"* in and through the work of your hands. How is your life a shining example to those in your sphere of influence?

Consider what courageous steps you need to take to more fully partner with Holy Spirit. It's through this partnership that you can realize the beautiful concept of co-creating with Creator God—living out His divinely appointed plans and purposes for your life and for those around you.

Seek Holy Spirit's guidance on how to cultivate a deep and intimate relationship with your Creator; ask those difficult questions and wait on His response.

Deep calleth unto deep, so each one of us can go deeper still in our relationship with the One who lovingly calls us by name.

In Romans 8:21 (NKJV), it is written *"because the creation itself also will be delivered from the bondage of corruption into the glorious liberty of the children of God"*.

We are called to be deliverers with Christ Jesus; may we echo the redemptive roar of freedom to those we have been called to impact and influence!

Key Takeaways

1. Search out Holy Spirit's guidance and direction in all aspects of your life, including your goals, dreams, and aspirations.

2. Spend time with Holy Spirit in worship, prayer, and meditation; study His life-giving Word.

3. Ask Holy Spirit those difficult questions that are weighing you down – we are being called to co-create with Him; do you know specifically what you have been called to co-create? He will tell you and guide you.

In Proverbs 5:3 (NIV) we read these life-giving words, "In the morning Lord, you hear my voice: in the morning I lay my requests before you and wait expectantly".

My challenge to you, dear Lioness, is to do the same, speak to your loving Creator in the morning, tell Him of your love for Him and worship Him; then lay down your requests before Him and wait with an expectant heart that He will answer. In His own time and in His own way!

Worship, prayer and waiting on the Lord, creates Divine Alignment between the Creator and His Creation; us.

We are called to command our morning, to speak out His Word and declare His plans and purposes for our lives – His Word can not return to Him void. As we declare His Word and co-partner with Him, His work will be established and accomplished in and through our lives.

Creator God, our Majestic Father, we praise You as King of Kings and Lord of Lords! Your Holy Word says that everything that has breath, praise the Lord! We praise You and only You. Thank you for not despising the days of our small beginnings Lord, but for walking with us every step of the way. We thank You that You are individually teaching each one of us the sound of Your Voice and our unique R.O.A.R. Give us ears to hear the instructions you us giving us and the wisdom and courage to both listen and obey.

In Jesus' Name, Amen.

การ R.O.A.R. of Reflection, Revelation & Responsibility

—

The R.O.A.R. of Reflection, Revelation & Responsibility

How have you been called to partner with Creator God?

What is your Loving Creator inviting you to co-create, co-labor, and co-birth with Him?

What is He revealing/confirming to you?

....
....
....
....
....
....
....
....
....
....
....
....
....
....
....

What new commitment do you need to make today to see your purpose "established"?

Use the space below to capture Creative AHA's.

Use the space below to capture Creative AHA's.

Golden Key Three

We Are Created to R.O.A.R. With Purpose

In Zechariah 4:10 (NLT), it is written *"Do not despise these small beginnings, for the Lord rejoices to see the work begin"*.

Refining Your R.O.A.R.
- Reflection • Revelation • Responsibility

> **We are created — prompted, made, established — to R.O.A.R. with purpose.**

Our 'in the beginning' design was to be a mirror image of our Creator here on earth, and we must see our work as a way of honoring our Creator God.

When we discover our R.O.A.R., we come into divine agreement with the redemptive roar/sound of Heaven, the sound of our Creator, our Abba Father.

The enemy has done everything he can think of to keep us silent, separate, and even scared; but no more. It is time to draw a line in the sand and appeal the Courts of Heaven to assign a restraining order to the works of the enemy; both in our individual lives and purpose, as well as in our families.

Now, more than ever, we must rise in both our faith and our fierceness and operate from a position of knowing, accepting, believing, and acting on the fact that we were made for more. We must do the work necessary to discover the sound that only we can make. Our sound — contribution, impact, influence — is much like our fingerprint, it is 100% uniquely ours. No one else can fulfill the assignments and destiny that is ours, it is unique to us.

That unique gift, therefore, also comes with responsibility. We must learn to steward the gift we have been given, our spiritual gifts as well as our talents and abilities given to us by the Giver of all Good Gifts, gifts that need to be shared with the world around us.

Fortunately, the prophet Zechariah encourages us not to "*despise these small beginnings*". Can't you just picture our loving, adoring Abba rejoicing over us as He sees us taking steps forward, no matter how short or long our stride.

He is truly, so loving, so patient, and so kind!

What does it mean to Own My Day, Own My R.O.A.R.?

RECOGNIZE: What do you love to do? What are you naturally good at? What can you do all day, every day that energizes you and brings you life, joy, passion, and energy?

OWN: What do other people applaud you for? What areas are you repeatedly asked to serve in? Which gifts are you called upon to use, most often?

ACTIVATE: What skills, talents, abilities, and spiritual gifts tie together what you love to do and create a platform for you? What can you get paid to do, that you love to do?

RELEASE: How can these gifts and talents serve and impact the world around you? What needs do you see in the world today that you were designed to be a solution for?

Let me share a secret with you — you, yes you, fierce, faith-filled Lioness — you, were set apart before you were ever born! It's a fact. Accept it and walk in the truth of who and Whose, you are!

You were set apart for Greatness before you were even born!

In Jeremiah 1:5a (NIV), it is written, *"Before I formed you in the womb I knew you, before you were born, I set you apart"*.

Key Takeaways

1. Owning Your R.O.A.R. is rooted in intimacy with Creator God. Spend time with Holy Spirit and seek to discern the sound of His Voice above all other voices.

2. Engage in rest and practice the art of stillness. As we rest and permit ourselves to take time to be still, we give ourselves permission to listen and receive the Divine Downloads that are ours to receive.

3. Invite Holy Spirit to speak to you, to reveal Father God's heart of love towards you and to illuminate your unique identity and purpose as per His original, 'in the beginning' intent and design.

By learning to **Own Your Day, Own Your Roar**, we come into proper alignment with God's unique plan for our lives and begin to create the impact and influence we were designed to have in the world around us.

Jeremiah 29:11 (NIV) explains it like this, *"For I know the plan I have for you," declares the Lord, "plans to prosper you and not to harm you, plans to give you hope and a future".*

The act of surrendering our own plans and desires to God, is an act of humility and obedience that will spiritually align our will with His Perfect Will for our lives. Trust that He knows what is best, that His timing is best, and that His plans are perfect. Surrendering allows us to partner with God and tap into His Supernatural wisdom and guidance in our lives. It is our Superpower, so to speak!

Creator God, our Blessed Father, thank you for choosing 'ahead of time' to R.O.A.R. through us, Your Creation, Your Daughters. May we bring You great Honor, Glory, and Praise as we learn to surrender our will to Your Perfect Will and Way in our lives.

Grant us the grace to partner wholeheartedly with You and receive Your Divine Revelation to **Recognize, Own, Activate**, and **Release** the unique identity and destiny You have for each one of us. Give us ears to hear Your Voice above all other voices in this season and the courage required to take the next best step forward.

In Jesus' Name, Amen.

The R.O.A.R. of Reflection, Revelation & Responsibility

Recognize:
What do you love to do?
What are you naturally good at?

What can you do all day, every day that energizes you and brings you life, joy, passion, and energy?

....

....

....

....

....

....

....

....

....

....

....

....

....

....

....

OWN:
What do other people applaud you for?
What areas are you repeatedly asked to serve in?

Which gifts are you called upon to use, most often?

ACTIVATE:

What skills, talents, abilities, and spiritual gifts tie together with what you love to do and create a platform for you to earn a profit?

What can you get paid to do, that you love to do?

Release

How can your gifts and talents serve and impact the world around you?

....
....
....
....
....
....
....
....
....
....
....
....
....
....
....
....

What needs do you see in the world today that you were designed to be a solution for?

Use the space below to capture Creative AHA's.

Use the space below to capture Creative AHA's.

Golden Key Four

We Are Commissioned to Fulfill Our Unique Destiny

In Ephesians 2:10 (TPT), it is written *"We have become his poetry, re-created people that will fulfill the destiny he has given each of us, for we are joined to Jesus, the Anointed One. Even before we were born, God planned our destiny and the good works we would do to fulfill it"*.

Refining Your R.O.A.R.
- Reflection • Revelation • Responsibility

> **We are commissioned — appointed, selected, assigned — to fulfill a unique destiny.**

The beautiful Greek word used here is "poiema", which translated gives us the word "poem" or "poetry". Our lives are meant to be lived as beautiful poetry for our God, poetry that will speak forth all that He commissioned to see fulfilled in our lives. As a writer, I love the beauty of words and the innate rhythm words can have as they are skillfully woven together.

Words create an emotional response; words convey passion and are used to express the things we hold close to our hearts.

Poetry is often an eloquent expression of that which we hold dearest; how meaningful it is that *"we have (therefore) become his poetry... joined to Jesus, the Anointed One"*; called to be the essence and very fulfillment of all God selected us to do before we were even born.

As we fulfill that destiny and complete those good works — we live out the love-story of becoming His poetry, His re-created people!

These good works allow us to live from a place of adoration, love, and intimacy with our Creator, fulfilling His calling and purpose for our lives and bringing Him great joy. As we yield to His Divine shaping, molding, and pruning, and commit to living out our prearranged destiny; we become His poetry and will be rewarded for simply doing what He created us 'ahead of time' to do.

Pause for a moment, close your eyes, and listen deeply with the ears of your heart to the scripture verses above. We have become His poetry, a re-created people, His Own perfected masterpieces, that will — not may, not should, but will — fulfill the destiny He has given each one of us.

We are not promised that it will always be easy as we seek to live out our callings, but we are promised that we are co-heirs with Jesus and if we share in His suffering, we will also share in His glory.

In Romans 8:16-17 (AMP), it is written *"The Spirit Himself testifies and confirms together with our spirit [assuring us] that we [believers] are children of God. And if [we are His] children, [then we are His] heirs also; heirs of God and fellow heirs with Christ [sharing His spiritual blessing and inheritance], if indeed we share in His suffering so that we may also share in His glory"*.

It is our choice to co-partner with Holy Spirit; He has already made us His co-heirs with Jesus, but we will need His guidance and support to stay on the path of purpose and righteousness. It is our choice, to live our lives in an extraordinary partnership with our Creator and King.
Our choice.

Ponder that. Breathe in the beauty and significance of it. Breathe out all doubt, fear, and lack of belief. Breathe in (YAH), breathe out (WEH). He is the very air we breathe. YAHWEH, *"I am who I am"* as it is written in Exodus 3:14 (NIV).

You were made for this precise moment in time. You are not an accident; you were created for such a time as this.

In Isaiah 43:1 (ESV), it is written *"But now thus says the Lord, he who created you, O Jacob, he who formed you, O Israel: "Fear not, for I have redeemed you; I have called you by name, you are mine".*

"You are mine". Allow the full impact of this promise to wash over you; to encircle and surround you. He loves us with an everlasting love. Permit His thoughts about you to become your thoughts about yourself. Receive the identity He has for you.

In Psalms 139:1 (TPT), it is written *"Lord, you know everything there is to know about me".*

Everything. Every single detail. Dear Lionesses, you are fearfully and wonderfully made, and utterly adored by your Creator!

Key Takeaways

1. Invite Holy Spirit to show you the Creator's marvelous pre-arranged plan for your life.

2. Engage in active questioning and listening with Holy Spirit; as we ask, we will receive the guidance and instruction we need.

3. Ask Holy Spirit to show you your current assignment and teach you how to complete it well. We are His Masterpieces and He has called us to go from Glory to Glory with Him.

Psalms 139:2-6 & 13-16 (TPT) goes on to say, "You perceive every movement of my heart and soul, and you understand my every thought before it even enters my mind. You are so intimately aware of me, Lord. You read my heart like an open book, and you know all the words I'm about to speak before I even start a sentence! You know every step I will take before my journey even begins. You've gone into my future to prepare the way, and in kindness, you follow behind me to spare me from the harm of my past. You have laid your hand on me! This is just too wonderful, deep, and incomprehensible! Your understanding of me brings me wonder and strength".

Creator God, you love us with an everlasting love that is without limits and boundaries! Grant us Dear Savior, the wisdom and grace to accept Your Love and to steward our days, our gifts and talents with intent and excellence. Teach us how to become the Masterpieces You have created us to be; to become Your poetry and Your re-created people and to bring You great Glory through both our heartfelt surrender and through the work of our hands.

In Jesus' Name, Amen.

The R.O.A.R. of Reflection,
Revelation & Responsibility

What beautiful poetry is currently being written through your life?

What 'Masterpiece' is yet to be written?

What is the next best step you can take to co-partner with Holy Spirit in the creation of this 'Masterpiece'?

....

....

....

....

....

....

....

....

....

....

....

....

....

....

....

Use the space below to capture Creative AHA's.

Use the space below to capture Creative AHA's.

Golden Key Five

We Are Conceived to Co-Labor and Co-Birth Destiny Babies

In John 16:21 (NIV), it is written *"A woman giving birth to a child has pain because her time has come, but when her baby is born, she forgets the anguish because of the joy that a child is born into the world"*.

We are designed to birth **Destiny Babies.**

Refining Your R.O.A.R.
● Reflection ● Revelation ● Responsibility

> **We are conceived — envisioned, imagined, planned — to co-labor, and co-birth with our Creator God.**

We are designed to birth **Destiny Babies**. Yes, you read that correctly. We are designed — impregnated with purpose — to birth ideas, inventions, songs, books, businesses, ministries, the list is endless. And yes, the birthing of **Destiny Babies** can also be painful; but when birthed, we too will forget the anguish and experience the joy of the fruit and increase of our labor.

In the ancient Near East, it was a tradition that up to three women would gather around the birthing woman. Each of these three women would have a function or role to perform in the natural realm of the birthing process; but they also carried a spiritual function or role which was to bless and empower the birthing woman with encouragement and wisdom.

How powerful. How practical.
How prophetic.

In Exodus 1:15-17 and 20-21 (NLT), *we meet two Hebrew midwives, let's consider their story: "Then Pharaoh, the king of Egypt, gave this order to the Hebrew midwives, Shiphrah and Puah: "When you help the Hebrew women as they give birth, watch as they deliver. If the baby is a boy, kill him; if it is a girl, let her live." But because the midwives feared God, they refused to obey the king's orders, they allowed the boys to live, too".*

Verses 20-21 *"So God was good to the midwives, and the Israelites continued to multiply, growing more and more powerful. And because the midwives feared God, he gave them families of their own".*

I love this story for several reasons, one, it demonstrates the favor we receive when we operate in the fear — reverence — of the Lord; and two, as it gives us a clear reminder that birthing doesn't happen on its own.

Birthing is designed to happen in community; or, to put it a slightly different way, in 'common unity'.

Birthing by nature, is cyclical. From a Spiritual perspective, one moment, you may be becoming larger and larger as the **Destiny Baby** you carry grows inside of you and you prepare for the time of delivery.

In one moment, you may find yourself in the role of a midwife, using your wisdom, experience, and understanding to help steward the seed within another woman. As a mentor, coach, or encourager, you'll support the growth, development, and strengthening of that seed as she prepares to give birth.

We must understand the season we are in, ready to release a sound of joyful expectation and hope when the time is right. Likewise, we should be prepared to offer mature wisdom and exhortation, encouraging those to whom we are assigned.

In James 1:17 (ESV), it is written *"Every good gift and every perfect gift is from above, coming down from the Father of lights, with whom there is no variation or shadow due to change"*.

Key Takeaways

1. We are conceived 'ahead of time' to co-create, co-labor, and co-birth **Destiny Babies.**

2. Birthing wasn't designed to happen on its own, but rather in the strength, support, and encouragement of a strong Kingdom community.

3. Every good and perfect gift **(Destiny Baby)** comes from our Creator God who is the Giver of all good gifts.

Have You Been Praying for Your Destiny Babies?

We must know the season that we are in. We are either creating, carrying, or birthing; or we are coming alongside a sister who herself, is creating, carrying, or birthing. There is always a role for us to play. I encourage you to pray for both your **Destiny Babies** and the ones you are a midwife to, just as you pray for your natural children.

In 1 Samuel 1:27 (ESV), it is written *"For this child, I prayed, and the Lord granted me my petition that I made to him"*.

In Luke 1:37 (NKJV), it is written *"For with God nothing will be impossible"*.

In Luke 1:45 (NKJV), it is written *"Blessed is she who believed, for there will be a fulfillment of those things which were told her from the Lord"*.

Creator God, our Heavenly Father, thank You for creating us to be impregnated with the seeds of destiny. Thank You for choosing to co-create, co-labor, and co-birth **Destiny Babies** with us, Your Daughters. We entrust both our **Destiny Babies** and the timing of their birth into Your Loving, Capable Hands! You are Alpha and Omega, our Beginning, and our End. We again surrender our will, our timing, our desires to Your Perfect Will, Timing and Plan for our lives. We choose to link arms with You, Abba Father and with those You have sent for us to be in community with, so that we can genuinely birth, develop, fulfill, and celebrate the purpose You have for each of our lives.

In Jesus' Name, Amen.

The R.O.A.R. of Reflection, Revelation & Responsibility

What Destiny Baby are you currently pregnant with? What are you carrying?

....

....

....

....

....

....

....

....

....

....

....

....

....

....

....

What dream, vision, idea and/or plan needs to be birthed through you in this season?

Who are your midwives? (Mentors/Coaches/Cheerleaders).

Who are you called to be a midwife for?

Use the space below to capture Creative AHA's.

Use the space below to capture Creative AHA's.

Golden Key Six

We Are Charged to Humble and Surrender Ourselves

In Luke 14:11 (NLT), it is written *"For those who exalt themselves will be humbled, and those who humble themselves will be exalted"*.

Our decision to humble ourselves draws the very Presence and Favor of Creator God, our Father, who loves to see His Beloved Children walking in a lifestyle of absolute submission and obedience to His Word.

Refining Your R.O.A.R.
• Reflection • Revelation • Responsibility

> **We are charged — impassioned, ardent, enthusiastic — to humble and surrender ourselves to God's plan and purpose for our lives.**

As we cultivate a lifestyle of full surrender, we create an atmosphere that allows us to host the very Presence of God which ultimately leads us in the fulfillment of His perfect plan and purpose for our lives.

In James 4:6-7 (NLT), *we are exhorted by James himself that God gives grace generously. As the Scriptures say, "God opposes the proud but gives grace to the humble." So, humble yourselves before God. Resist the devil, and he will flee from you".*

Personally, I have learned—sometimes the hard way—that surrender is powerful. The more I entrust every thought, fear, concern, dream, and seed of hope to the Throne of Grace, the more my faith and focus grow in strength and resilience.

Abba Father, who knows me inside and out, simply comes and fills me with more of Him; more, of His Glory, His Strength, His Power, and most importantly, more of His Love.

In Zephaniah 3:16-17 (MSG), it is written *"Your God is present among you, a strong Warrior there to serve you. Happy to have you back, he'll calm you with his love and delight you with his songs"*.

In the New Living Translation (NLT), it is written *"He will take delight in you with gladness. With his love, he will calm all your fears. He will rejoice over you with joyful songs"*.

Can you hear His songs? Songs of love, adoration, encouragement, hope, peace, revelation, and even strategy, and blueprints. A beautiful, melodic symphony and perhaps at times a celebratory clap of shouts and cheers as our Cloud of Witnesses and Angelic Host join in!

Key Takeaways

1. Our decision to humble ourselves and obey, brings our Creator great joy and results in Him singing His Songs over us.

2. The Word of God is very clear that *"God opposes the proud but gives grace to the humble"*. Our response of obedience should be equally clear — who wouldn't want grace versus opposition?

3. We are victorious, triumphant when we surrender and partner with Creator God.

In Psalms 42:7-8 (ESV), we are assured that *"Deep calls to deep at the roar of your waterfalls; all your breakers and your waves have gone over me. By day the Lord commands his steadfast love, and at night his song is with me, a prayer to the God of my life"*.

How glorious! The joy and promises embedded in these verses come as a direct result of us choosing to humble ourselves to the Will of our Creator.

In 1 Peter 5:6 (NLT), it is written *"So humble yourselves under the mighty power of God, and at the right time He will lift you up in honor"*.

In Jeremiah 10:23 (NLT), it is written, *"I know, Lord, that our lives are not our own. We are not able to plan our own course"*.

Thankfully, the Word also say in Psalms 23 (TPT), that *"The Lord is my best friend and my shepherd. I always have more than enough. He offers a resting place for me in his luxurious love. His tracks take me to an oasis of peace, the quiet brook of bliss. That's where he restores and revives my life. He opens before me the pathways to God's pleasure and leads me along in his footsteps of righteousness so that I can bring honor to his name. Lord, even when your path takes me through the valley of deepest darkness, fear will never conquer me, for you already have! You remain close to me and lead me through it all the way. Your authority is my strength and peace. The comfort of your love takes away my fear. I'll never be lonely, for you are near. You become my delicious feast even when my enemies dare to fight. You anoint me with the fragrance of your Holy Spirit; you give me all I can drink of you until my heart overflows. So why would I fear the future? For your goodness and love pursue me all the days of my life. Then afterward, when my life is through, I'll return to your glorious presence to be forever with you!"*.

A Heavenly R.O.A.R.

A Heavenly R.O.A.R. — a triumphant sound of victory, and freedom as we choose day by day to press in. Our greatest source of encouragement, wisdom and instruction is quite simply, the Word of God.

Here are a few additional treasures:

In Hosea 11:10 (NLT), it is written *"For someday the people will follow me. I, the Lord, will roar like a lion. And when I roar, my people will return trembling from the west"*.

Let's not wait, let's return and follow Him today!

In Psalms 27:8 (NLT), it is written *"My heart has heard you say, "Come and talk with me." And my heart responds, "Lord, I am coming"."*

Who will join me in saying, "Lord, I am coming"?

Creator God, our Loving and Gracious Father, we thank You for Your awe-inspiring Love, Grace, and Mercy towards us Your Children, Your Daughters. We thank You for calming us with Your Love. We thank You for delighting us with Your Songs. We thank You that Victory is ours when we surrender and partner with You. We thank You that every resource we need is found in You, in the center of Your Love and that all of Heaven rejoices to see our work begin.

In Jesus' Name, Amen.

The R.O.A.R. of Reflection, Revelation & Responsibility

Can you hear His Songs being sung over you?

What do you sense that Holy Spirit is inviting you to surrender in this season?

What response is required of you?

Use the space below to capture Creative AHA's.

Use the space below to capture Creative AHA's.

Golden Key Seven

We Are Convoked to Release a Multi-Generational Remnant-R.O.A.R.

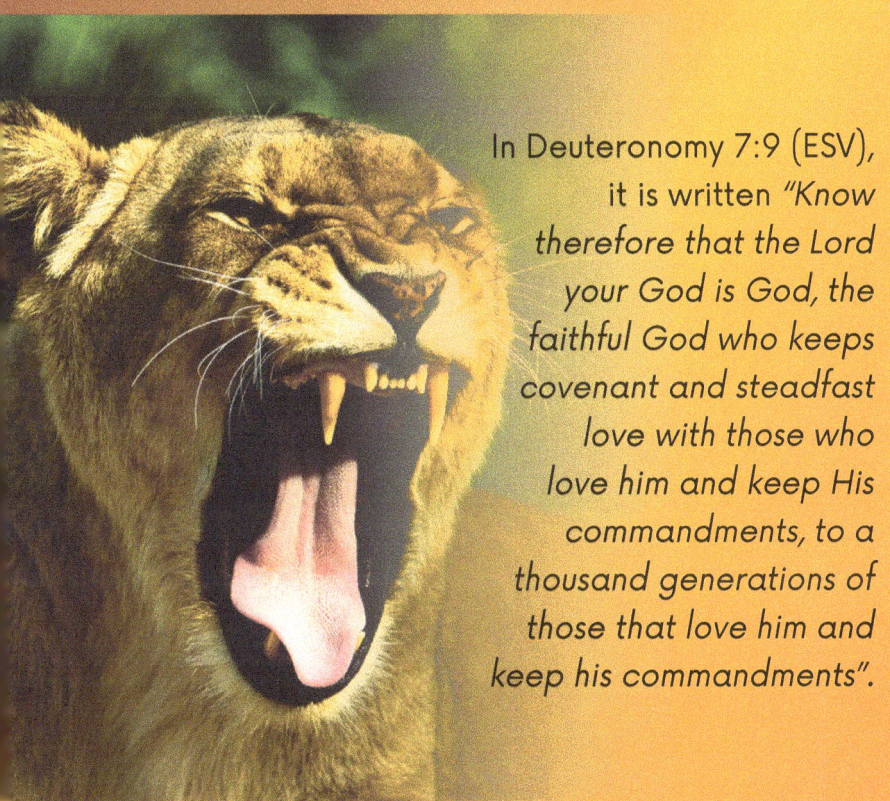

In Deuteronomy 7:9 (ESV), it is written "Know therefore that the Lord your God is God, the faithful God who keeps covenant and steadfast love with those who love him and keep His commandments, to a thousand generations of those that love him and keep his commandments".

Refining Your R.O.A.R.
- Reflection
- Revelation
- Responsibility

> **We are convoked — summoned, assembled, and gathered — to release a multi-generational Remnant-R.O.A.R.**

God will use us, to release a multi-generational Remnant-R.O.A.R. that will call all of Creation back to the Creator Himself.

Our entire purpose is to point others towards the Cross and towards a personal, intimate, and life-changing relationship with our Lord and Savior, Jesus Christ.

In Job 37:2-5 (NIV), it is written *"Listen! Listen to the roar of his voice, to the rumbling that comes from his mouth. He unleashes his lightning beneath the whole heaven and sends it to the ends of the earth. After that comes the sound of his roar; he thunders with his majestic voice. When his voice resounds, he holds nothing back. God's voice thunders in marvelous ways; he does great things beyond our understanding".*

There is a supernatural release of Power when we unite with one another and with our Creator. With this Power and Authority, we will co-create what has been assigned to us. It will be used to impact and influence the world in which we live. Through this Power, the hearts and souls of those we love, as well as those we have been called to minister to, will be brought into a right relationship with Creator God.

We must be willing to embrace the risk of stepping out, stepping up, and stepping into our God-given destinies.

The prayers we have prayed and continue to pray are being heard and answered. We will see our households saved. We will see revival. We will see families, churches, communities, governments, and nations transformed. We will be a part of that transformational process when we choose to walk out the purpose which only, we can fulfill.

Key Takeaways

1. As we the remnant choose to discover, develop, and unleash our R.O.A.R., we will see a fulfillment of John 14:12-14, greater works.

2. We are God's secret weapon prepared in the secret place, for a time such as this.

3. Lionesses hunt in packs, with great stealth, skill, and intent; we need one another to fulfill our Kingdom assignments.

May our hearts echo the words in Psalms 90:16-17 (TPT), *"Let us see your miracles again, and let the rising generation see the glorious wonders you're famous for. O Lord our God, let your sweet beauty rest upon us. Come work with us, and then our works will endure; you will give us success in all we do"*.

We must be willing to unite and release our unified R.O.A.R.

As we unite and release our powerful, unified, multi-generational R.O.A.R., we will see an outpour of miracles and glorious signs and wonders!

In John 14:12-14 (NLT), it is written *"I tell you the truth, anyone who believes in me will do the same works I have done, and even greater works, because I am going to be with the Father. You can ask for anything in my name, and I will do it, so that the Son can bring glory to the Father. Yes, ask me for anything in my name, and I will do it!'*.

It is time to release our powerful, united, multi-Generational R.O.A.R.!

In Micah 5:8a (NLT), it is written *"The remnant left in Israel will take their place among the nations. They will be like a lion among the animals of the forest, like a strong young lion among flocks of sheep and goats..."*.

It is time to take our places. Our destinies are both inter and cross-sectional; we need each other, and we need to work together, serve together and R.O.A.R. together to achieve the greater works that Jesus spoke of.

We have intersectional destinies and we are designed to release a united R.O.A.R.

As you may already know, lionesses are the main providers of food for their pride, and they hunt together in a pack. For the pride to survive both the Lion and the Lioness must know and operate in their own unique role. Both are required for survival, growth, and multiplication of the pride. Together their strength and their power are unstoppable and unmatched.

The same applies to the Body of Christ.

We, His Bride, must learn to celebrate one another, to come alongside one another and support one another; as we do, we will also be unstoppable as we advance Heaven's multi-generational Remnant-R.O.A.R. here on earth!

Creator God, our Roaring Lion of Judah, we thank You for creating us as Your secret weapon for a time such as this. Thank You that Your Word says in Psalms 38:9 (TPT), that *"My tears are liquid words, and you can read them all"*. You have heard every cry, every word, every prayer. You have prepared us in secret to be used for Your perfect plans and purposes. We choose today to join forces with You in a fresh way, with a fresh understanding of the importance of our united Remnant-R.O.A.R., holding nothing back so that You receive all the Glory, Honor and Fame.

In Jesus' Name, Amen.

The R.O.A.R. of Reflection, Revelation & Responsibility

What do you want to be the legacy of your multi-generational R.O.A.R.?

....

....

....

....

....

....

....

....

....

....

....

....

....

....

Who will it influence and impact; how do you want it to echo in eternity?

What steps do you need to take to implement and activate these 7 Golden Keys in your life today?

....

....

....

....

....

....

....

....

....

....

....

....

....

....

....

....

How will that activation impact your sphere of influence — family, community, church, nation?

Use the space below to capture Creative AHA's.

Use the space below to capture Creative AHA's.

Noteworthy Ideas

Personal Message from the Author

Own Your Day, Own Your Roar, is a message of hope, inspiration, and activation that Holy Spirit shared with me and instructed me to share with you.

The Roaring 2020s Brand was conceived in September 2019. This was during the Rosh Hashanah 'head of the year' celebration for the new decade of 5780. This decade is known as the Decade of Pey, a word often translated to mean sound or voice. I was inquiring of the Lord about the sound He wanted me to make in this new decade.

My thoughts turned to the Roaring 20s from a hundred years ago. I considered what sound we were to make globally in this new era of The Roaring 2020s. In my mind's eye, I saw the Roaring Lion of Judah, roaring through the face of humanity. I heard in my spirit, 'It is a decade of the Creator and His Creation, co-creating.'

The logo that represents the brand is what I saw that day. From that encounter, The Roaring 2020s brand was born. Subsequently **'Own Your Day, Own Your Roar'** platforms were also birthed.

Our R.O.A.R. is both a message and a mantle. It empowers us to **Recognize, Own, Activate,** and **Release** our unique sound. We are to walk out our God-given purpose with integrity and confidence. We know it is His Power working within us and because of that, we are already victorious!

If you are reading this book and have never invited Jesus Christ to become your Lord and Savior, today is the day of salvation!

I invite you to pray with me:

> Dear Jesus, I know that I am a sinner, in need of a Savior, and I choose today to ask for Your forgiveness and Your salvation. I believe you died for my sins and rose from the dead to be the Savior of the world. I choose to accept the identity and destiny You have for me and put you first, to serve you. I welcome Your forgiveness and Your salvation today.
>
> In the Precious Name of Jesus Christ, Amen.

If you prayed that prayer of salvation today, let me be the first to say,

'Welcome to the Family!'

Please take a moment to reach out to me at korrie@ownyourdayownyourroar.com. Whether you wish to share a testimony or send a prayer request, I am here to connect with you further.

Afterword

If you feel you haven't found your R.O.A.R. yet, or you need more help refining your unique purpose, know that you are not alone.

Entrepreneur and Business Coach, Korrie L Silver helps women to unlock the R.O.A.R. in their hearts and become the Lionesses they were created to be.

Connect with Korrie:

www.korriesilver.com
www.ownyourdayownyourroar.com

About the Author

As a Marketplace Minister, Transformational Coach and Business Strategist, Korrie has a keen eye for identifying gaps and developing innovative strategies and solutions for growth and breakthrough for her clients. Coaching sessions will simultaneously consider both your inner and outer game and identity beliefs and behaviors that are holding you back from the success and breakthrough you were created to have.

Together you will **Recognize, Own, Activate,** and **Release** your God-given identity and purpose, breaking through limitations and embracing new ways of thinking.

The **Own Your Day, Own Your Roar** platform is designed to support you in your journey toward personal and professional growth, with a strong foundation in faith.

Thank You for Reading My Book!

I truly appreciate your feedback and enjoy hearing your thoughts.

Could you please spare two minutes to leave a helpful review on Amazon? I'd love to know what you thought about the book.

Thank you!

Korrie L Silver

www.ingramcontent.com/pod-product-compliance
Lightning Source LLC
Chambersburg PA
CBHW041317110526
44591CB00021B/2815